LEVEL

1

Dinosaurs

Kathleen Weidner Zoehfeld

NATIONAL GEOGRAPHIC

Washington, D.C.

For Whitley

Library of Congress Cataloging-in-Publication Data
Zoehfeld, Kathleen Weidner.
Dinosaurs / by Kathleen W. Zoehfeld.
p. cm.
ISBN 978-1-4263-0775-1 (pbk. : alk. paper) -- ISBN 978-1-4263-0776-8 (library binding : alk. paper)
1. Dinosaurs--Juvenile literature. I. Title.
QE861.5.Z63 2011
567.9--dc22
2010037806

All illustrations by Franco Tempesta unless otherwise noted below:
5, 32 (bottom, left): © Will Van Overbeek/ NationalGeographicStock.com; 6-9, 23, 32 (bottom, right): © Louie Psihoyos/ Corbis; 11 (top, left): © Brooks Walker/ NationalGeographicStock.com; 11 (top, right): © Xu Xing; 18: © James Leynse/ Corbis; 20: © Francois Gohier/ Photo Researchers, Inc.; 26-27: © Karel Havlicek/ NationalGeographicStock.com; 28: © Joel Sartore/ NationalGeographic-Stock.com; 29: © National Geographic/ NationalGeographicStock.com; 31: © Paul Bricknell/Dorling Kindersley/ Getty Images; 32 (top, right): © Lynn Johnson/ NationalGeographicStock.com

**National Geographic supports K–12 educators with ELA Common Core Resources.
Visit natgeoed.org/commoncore for more information.**

Printed in the United States of America
Paperback: 15/WOR/6
RLB: 15/WOR/5

Table of Contents

Big Scary Bones!

Have you ever seen dinosaur bones in a museum (mew-ZEE-um)? Some of them are huge! If those bones came to life, it would be pretty scary.

But not to worry. All the big, scary dinosaurs died off long, long ago.

The bones weren't always at the museum. Where did they come from?

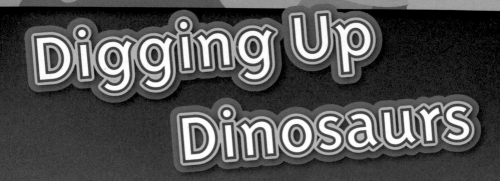

Digging Up Dinosaurs

The dinosaur bones were buried safely in rock for a long time.

The bones are fossils (FOS-uls). Paleontologists (pay-lee-on-TOL-o-jists) found them. They dug them out of the ground.

Word Bites

FOSSIL: Part of a living thing that has been saved in stone

PALEONTOLOGIST: A scientist who finds and studies fossils

They brought the fossil bones
to the museum and cleaned them.
Then they put them all together.

Bones were on the inside of a
dinosaur. But what did dinosaurs
look like on the outside?

9

Dinosaur Skin

Sometimes dinosaur skin left prints in mud. The mud hardened and saved the prints.

These fossils tell us that some dinosaurs were scaly, like lizards.

Triceratops
(tri-SER-ah-tops)

skin fossil

feather fossil

And some dinosaurs had feathers, like birds.

Buitreraptor
(BWEE-tree-RAP-tore)

Dinosaur Superstars

Tyrannosaurus rex
(ty-RAN-oh-SORE-us REX) was one of the biggest meat-eaters that ever walked the Earth.

Diplodocus
(dih-PLOD-uh-kus) was one of the longest dinosaurs ever found.

Pachycephalosaurus
(pack-ee-SEF-ah-loh-SORE-us) walked on two legs and had a thick, domed head.

Triceratops

(tri-SER-a-tops) had a huge head with three large horns and a wide neck frill.

Ankylosaurus

(AN-kye-loh-SORE-us) was an armored dinosaur. It had a solid bone club at the end of its tail.

Stegosaurus

(STEG-oh-SORE-us) had rows of tall plates running down its back. Its tail had four deadly spikes.

Smallest Dinosaurs

When you go to the museum, be sure to look for the smallest dinosaurs.

Some are small enough to hold in your hands. Many small dinosaurs had feathers.

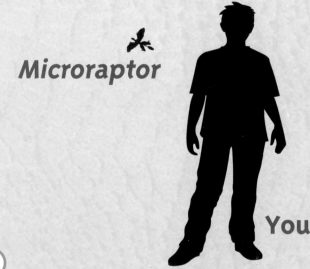

Microraptor

You

Microraptor
(MIKE-ro-rap-tore)

Biggest Dinosaurs

The biggest dinosaurs were the long-necked sauropods (SORE-uh-PODS). You can't miss them! Sauropods like *Argentinosaurus* are the biggest land animals that ever lived.

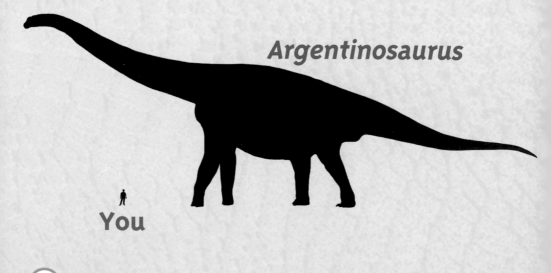

Argentinosaurus

You

Argentinosaurus
(ahr-gen-TEEN-oh-SORE-us)

Walking on Tiptoes

Big or small, scaly or feathery—all dinosaurs walked on their toes.

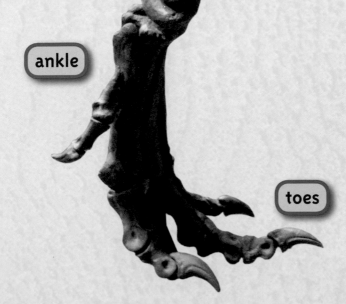

knee

ankle

toes

Q How do you know when there's a dinosaur under your bed?

A Your nose hits the ceiling!

And all dinosaurs had curvy, S-shaped necks.

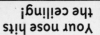

neck

Edmontosaurus

(ed-MON-toh-SORE-us)

What Did Dinosaurs Eat?

A dinosaur's teeth tell us what it ate. *Brachiosaurus* and *Diplodocus* were plant-eaters. They had dozens of chisel-like teeth. Their teeth were good for snipping tough branches.

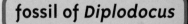

fossil of *Diplodocus*

Brachiosaurus

(BRACK-ee-oh-SORE-us)

Deinonychus

(die-NON-e-kus)

Other dinosaurs were meat–eaters. They ate other animals.

Deinonychus had teeth as sharp as steak knives. They were perfect for slicing meat.

tooth of meat-eater
Tyrannosaurus rex

23

Dinosaur Moms and Babies

All dinosaurs, even the scariest meat-eaters, laid eggs and had babies.

Some of them, such as *Oviraptor*, guarded their nests and kept their eggs warm. When the babies hatched, the parents looked after them until they were big enough to live on their own.

Oviraptor
(OH-vih-RAP-tore)

Is THAT a Dinosaur?

Lots of people think anything big and dead is a dinosaur. But that's not right.

Is this a dinosaur?

woolly mammoth
(WOOL-ee MAM-uth)

No! The woolly mammoth was huge. But this animal did not lay eggs like a dinosaur. And it had fur. No dinosaurs had fur.

The woolly mammoth lived after the big dinosaurs went extinct (ik-STINKED).

Word Bites

EXTINCT: No longer alive. When all members of a group of animals are dead, they are extinct.

Is this a dinosaur?

Chicken
living dinosaur

It walks on its toes. It has a curvy neck. It has feathers like *Anchiornis*. And it lays eggs.

Yes! A chicken is a dinosaur. All birds are living dinosaurs.

Anchiornis
(ank-ee-OR-niss)
extinct dinosaur

Your Pet Dinosaur

Many people would love to keep dinosaurs as pets.

You might think a *Tyrannosaurus rex* would be fun to play fetch with. But you wouldn't want to be near it at dinnertime. And besides, it's extinct!

If you want a dinosaur of your own, look for one that's small. A small dinosaur makes a very good pet!

EXTINCT: No longer alive. When all members of a group of animals are dead, they are extinct.

FOSSIL: Part of a living thing that has been saved in stone

MUSEUM: A building where you can see dinosaurs and other rare and important things

PALEONTOLOGIST: A scientist who finds and studies fossils